Donuts
with
Dad

story
Margaret Bernstein

pictures
Lincoln Adams

Halo
PUBLISHING
INTERNATIONAL

ISBN: 978-1-61244-664-6
Library of Congress Control Number: 2018910197

Printed in the United States of America

Published by Halo Publishing International
1100 NW Loop 410
Suite 700 - 176
San Antonio, Texas 78213
1-877-705-9647
www.halopublishing.com
contact@halopublishing.com

This book is dedicated to my children,
Randy and Alex, and especially to my husband,
C. Randolph Keller, who inspires all my books
for dads. You would go to the ends of the earth
for your children and are living proof that
the fatherless cycle can be broken.
We are so grateful for your love.

Also, a thousand thanks to Steve Killpack of the
Healthy Fathering Collaborative of Cleveland,
for your unwavering support.

4

Have a seat, right over there.
Daddy's going to do your hair.
I'll get the hair clips and the brush.
We'll take our time, no need to rush.

I love your hair and the way it twirls.
I can braid it, twist it or give you curls.
I'm a master of styles. It's easy to see.
No dad around does it better than me.

Time to get dressed, so what will you wear?
A pink dress to match the bows in your hair?
Since we are going some special places,
put on your sneakers with the pink laces.

You look so pretty that it makes me think
there's nothing wrong with a dad wearing pink.
Stay right there and close your eyes.
Daddy's got a big surprise!

Now we both look great,
without a doubt.

Have a seat on
your throne.
It's all
decked out!

I've been thinking about
this for quite a while.
It's not every day Dad
goes to school with his child.

So I brought the things that a princess should have. Now that's what I call doing Donuts with Dad!

There's lots
of day left.
There's more
we could do.

Want to go to
the movies?
Go to the zoo?

We could go out to eat.
You'll be my guest.
I'll order the foods that
you like the best.

And when that's over,
we'll go out and play.
I brought extra clothes
to top off this day.

21

On the basketball court,
we'll show off our skills.
Shoot the ball like
I showed you.
We'll give them
a thrill.

22

We'll stop at the dog park
and see all the pets.

Then climb up a hill
and watch the sun set.
We had so much fun
jumping around

that your hair came loose.
It came tumbling down.
That's OK, baby.
We had a great day.

Tomorrow, I'll fix it a brand new way.
Slip under the covers. Good night! Sleep tight.
And know Daddy loves you with all his might.

26

CPSIA information can be obtained
at www.ICGtesting.com
Printed in the USA
BVHW062203021022
648493BV00007B/122

9 781612 446646